W9-BKA-941

Cool Italian Cooking

Fun and Tasty Recipes for Kids

Lisa Wagner

TO ADULT HELPERS

You're invited to assist up-and-coming chefs! As children learn to cook, they develop new skills, gain confidence, and make some delicious food. What's more, it's a lot of fun!

Efforts have been made to keep the recipes in this book authentic yet simple. You will notice that some of the recipes are more difficult than others. Be there to help children with these recipes, but encourage them to do as much as they can on their own. Also encourage them to try new foods and experiment with their own ideas. Building creativity into the cooking process encourages children to think like real chefs.

Before getting started, set some ground rules about using the kitchen, cooking tools, and ingredients. Most importantly, adult supervision is a must whenever a child uses the stove, oven, or sharp tools.

So, put on your aprons and stand by. Let your young chefs take the lead. Watch and learn. Taste their creations. Praise their efforts. Enjoy the culinary adventure!

visit us at www.abdopublishing.com

Published by ABDO Publishing Company, a division of ABDO, P.O. Box 398166, Minneapolis, Minnesota 55439. Copyright © 2011 by Abdo Consulting Group, Inc. International copyrights reserved in all countries. No part of this book may be reproduced in any form without written permission from the publisher. Checkerboard Library™ is a trademark and logo of ABDO Publishing Company.

Printed in the United States of America, North Mankato, Minnesota
102010
012011

 PRINTED ON RECYCLED PAPER

Design and Production: Colleen Dolphin, Mighty Media, Inc.
Art Direction: Colleen Dolphin
Series Editor: Liz Salzmann
Food Production: Frankie Tuminelly
Photo Credits: Colleen Dolphin, Photodisc, Shutterstock

The following manufacturers/names appearing in this book are trademarks: Crystal Farms®, Dei Fratelli®, Heinz®, Kemps®, Morton®, Pyrex®, Old London®, Target®

Wagner, Lisa, 1958-

Cool italian cooking : fun and tasty recipes for kids / Lisa Wagner.
    p. cm. -- (Cool world cooking)
Includes index.
ISBN 978-1-61714-661-9
1. Cooking, Italian--Juvenile literature. I. Title.
TX723.W18 2011
641.5945--dc22

2010022193

Table of Contents

Explore the Foods of Italy!

Do you like Italian food? Now you can learn to make it! Most people like spaghetti and meatballs. But they'll love the homemade **version** you can make from this book!

Food is very important in Italy. Dinners take hours to prepare and eat! The dinner table is the center of family life. Family meals often include grandparents, uncles, aunts, and **cousins**. "Put the love in the food" is a popular saying in Italy.

Many Italian cities and towns have outdoor markets that sell fresh foods. Northern Italy is known for its meats, cheeses, and grapes. Southern Italy is warmer. Vegetables, fruits, olives, and olive oil are produced there. Fish is harvested along the coasts of the Mediterranean and Adriatic Seas. Everything is fresh! Are you ready for a tasty Italian adventure? Put on your aprons and off we go!

GET THE PICTURE!

When a step number in a recipe has a dotted circle around it, look for the picture that goes with it. The circle around the photo will be the same color as the step number.

HOW DO YOU SAY THAT?

You may come across some Italian words you've never heard of in this book. Don't worry! There's a pronunciation guide on page 30!

The Basics

ASK PERMISSION

Before you cook, get permission to use the kitchen, cooking tools, and ingredients. When you need help, ask. Always get help when you use the stove or oven.

GET ORGANIZED

Being well organized is a chef's secret ingredient for success!

◉ Read through the entire recipe before you do anything else.

◉ Gather all your cooking tools and ingredients.

◉ Get the ingredients ready. The list of ingredients tells how to prepare each item.

◉ Put each prepared ingredient into a separate bowl.

◉ Read the recipe instructions carefully. Do the steps in the order they are listed.

GOOD COOKING TAKES PREP WORK

Many ingredients need preparation before they are used. Look at a recipe's ingredients list. Some ingredients will have words such as chopped, sliced, or grated next to them. These words tell you how to prepare the ingredients.

Give yourself plenty of time and be patient. Always wash fruits and vegetables. Rinse them well and pat them dry with a **towel**. Then they won't slip when you cut them. After you prepare each ingredient, put it in a separate prep bowl. Now you're ready!

BE SMART, BE SAFE

- If you use the stove or oven, you need an adult with you.

- Never use the stove or oven if you are home alone.

- Always get an adult to help with the hot jobs, such as frying with oil.

- Have an adult nearby when you are using sharp tools such as knives, peelers, graters, or food processors.

- Always turn pot handles to the back of the stove. This helps prevent accidents and spills.

- Work slowly and carefully. If you get hurt, let an adult know right away!

BE NEAT, BE CLEAN

- Start with clean hands, clean tools, and a clean work surface.

- Tie back long hair so it stays out of the way and out of the food.

- Roll up your sleeves.

- An apron will protect your clothes from spills and splashes.

- Chef hats are **optional**!

KEY SYMBOLS

In this book, you will see some symbols beside the recipes. Here is what they mean.

HOT STUFF!
The recipe requires the use of a stove or oven. You need adult assistance and supervision.

SUPER SHARP!
A sharp tool such as a peeler, knife, or grater is needed. Get an adult to stand by.

EVEN COOLER!
This symbol means adventure! Give it a try! Get inspired and invent your own cool ideas.

No Germs Allowed!

Raw eggs and raw meat have bacteria in them. These bacteria are killed when food is cooked. But they can survive out in the open and make you sick! After you handle raw eggs or meat, wash your hands, tools, and work surfaces with soap and water. Keep everything clean!

The Tool Box

A box on the bottom of the first page of each recipe lists the tools you need. When you come across a tool you don't know, turn back to these pages.

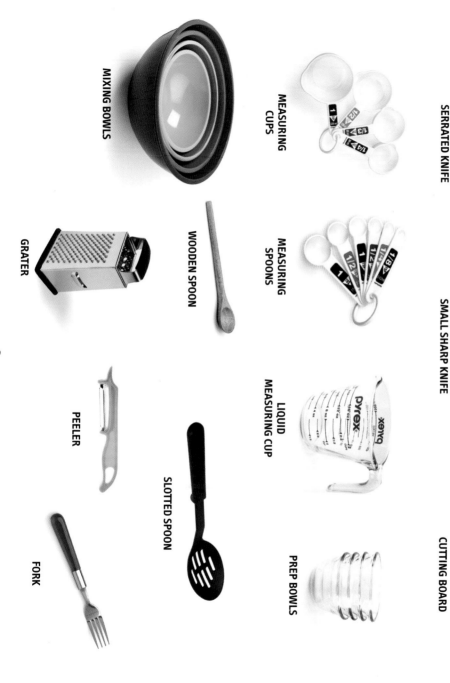

SERRATED KNIFE

SMALL SHARP KNIFE

CUTTING BOARD

MEASURING CUPS

MEASURING SPOONS

LIQUID MEASURING CUP

PREP BOWLS

MIXING BOWLS

WOODEN SPOON

GRATER

PEELER

SLOTTED SPOON

FORK

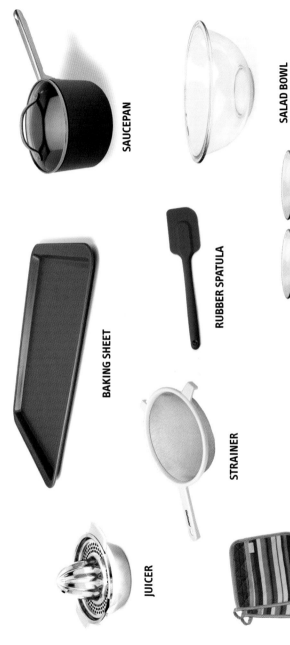

SAUCEPAN

SALAD BOWL

9 × 9-INCH BAKING DISH

SERVING BOWL

DESSERT BOWLS

RUBBER SPATULA

BAKING SHEET

HEAVY-BOTTOMED
SAUCEPAN

TIMER

STRAINER

FRYING PAN

JUICER

POT HOLDERS

ALUMINUM FOIL

ROUND GLASS
BAKING DISH

9

Cool Cooking Terms

Here are some basic cooking terms and the actions that go with them. Whenever you need a reminder, just turn back to these pages.

FIRST THINGS FIRST

Always wash fruit and vegetables well. Rinse them under cold water. Pat them dry with a **towel**. Then they won't slip when you cut them.

CHOP

Chop means to cut things into small pieces with a knife.

GRATE

Grate means to shred something into small pieces using a grater.

JUICE

To *juice* a fruit means to remove the juice from its insides by squeezing it or using a juicer.

SPREAD

Spread means to make a smooth layer with a spoon, knife, or spatula.

SLICE

Slice means to cut food into pieces of the same thickness.

MASH

Mash means to press down and smash food with a fork or potato masher.

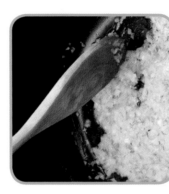

SAUTÉ

Sauté means to fry quickly in a pan using a small amount of oil or butter.

MINCE

Mince means to cut the food into the tiniest possible pieces. Garlic is often minced.

TOSS

Toss means to turn ingredients over to coat them with seasonings.

PEEL

Peel means to remove the skin, often with a peeler.

The Coolest Ingredients

TOMATO

RED BELL PEPPER

SCALLIONS

FIELD GREENS

CELERY

CARROTS

GREEN BEANS

SHALLOTS

LEMONS

WHITE ONION

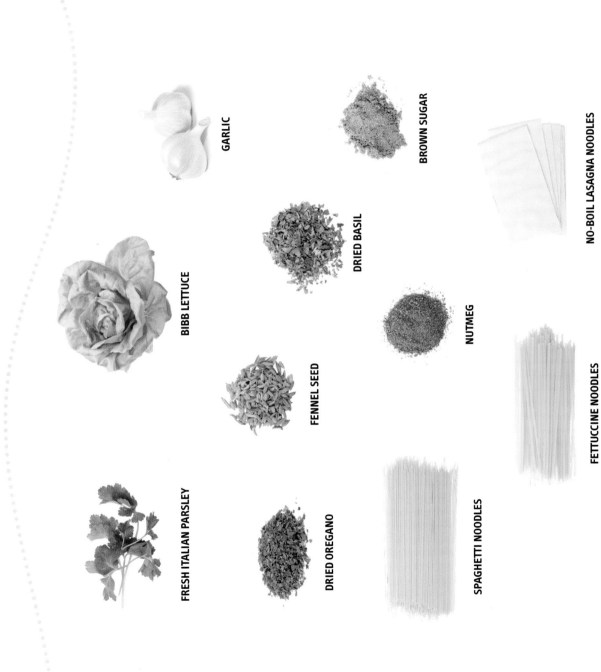

GARLIC

BROWN SUGAR

NO-BOIL LASAGNA NOODLES

DRIED BASIL

BIBB LETTUCE

NUTMEG

FENNEL SEED

FETTUCCINE NOODLES

FRESH ITALIAN PARSLEY

DRIED OREGANO

SPAGHETTI NOODLES

13

PARMESAN CHEESE

HEAVY WHIPPING CREAM

ITALIAN BREAD

EGG

BUTTER

MOZZARELLA CHEESE

GROUND BEEF

RICOTTA CHEESE

CRUSHED TOMATOES

ITALIAN SAUSAGE

Allergy Alert!

Some people have a reaction when they eat certain foods. If you have any allergies, you know what it's all about. An allergic reaction can require emergency medical help. Nut allergies can be especially **dangerous.** Before you serve anything made with nuts or peanut oil, ask if anyone has a nut allergy.

About Organic Foods

Organic foods are grown without **synthetic** fertilizers and **pesticides.** This is good for the earth. And recent studies show that organic foods may be more **nutritious** than **conventionally** grown foods.

Organic foods used to be hard to find. But now you can find organic **versions** of most foods. Organic foods are more expensive than conventionally grown foods. Families must decide for themselves whether to spend extra for organic foods.

OLIVE OIL

GROUND PEPPER

SUGAR

RED WINE VINEGAR

SALT

BREAD CRUMBS

Italian Extras

Take your Italian cooking to the next level! The ideas on these pages will show you how.

PERFECT PASTA EVERY TIME!

Different kinds of pasta have different cook times. The suggested cooking time is always on the package.

1 Put 4 quarts of water in a heavy-bottomed saucepan. Add 1 tablespoon of salt and stir until it is **dissolved**.

2 Bring the water to a boil over high heat. The entire surface of the water should be bubbling. Add the pasta and stir gently.

3 Wait for the water to begin boiling again. Then set the timer for the time shown on the package. Boil the pasta uncovered and stir it every few minutes. Make sure the pasta doesn't stick to the bottom of the pan.

4 Set a colander in the sink. Pour the pasta into the colander to drain. Serve immediately with sauce.

GORGEOUS GARLIC BREAD

Makes 8 to 12 servings

INGREDIENTS

18-inch loaf soft Italian bread
12 tablespoons softened butter
5 cloves garlic, minced
1 cup Parmesan cheese, grated

1 Preheat the oven to 350 degrees. Slice the bread lengthwise. Don't cut through all the way.

2 Mix the butter, garlic, and Parmesan cheese in a bowl. Spread the mixture evenly on both sides of the bread.

3 Close the loaf. Slice it into 1-inch pieces. Don't cut all the way through. Wrap the loaf in aluminum foil. Set it on a baking sheet. Bake for 15 minutes.

4 Carefully unwrap the bread and finish slicing though each cut to separate the pieces.

REMARKABLE RED SAUCE

Makes about 3 quarts

INGREDIENTS

2 tablespoons olive oil

1 pound bulk Italian sausage

1 large onion, chopped

3 cloves garlic, minced

3 28-ounce cans crushed tomatoes

¾ cup water

1 teaspoon fennel seed

1 teaspoon dried basil

1 teaspoon dried oregano

1 teaspoon salt

¼ teaspoon ground pepper

1 tablespoon brown sugar

Tip:
This sauce is popular, as it is in Naples, or Napoli, in Italy. For 1 pound of pasta. Freeze use 1 quart of sauce for up to three months!

1 Heat the olive oil in a large saucepan over medium heat. Add the sausage and break it up using a wooden spoon. Cook it until all the pink is gone.

2 Move the sausage to a bowl using a slotted spoon. Set it aside.

3 Add the onion and garlic to the saucepan and sauté for 5 minutes, stirring constantly.

4 Add the sausage to the onion and garlic.

5 Add the crushed tomatoes. Pour ¼ cup water into each can. Then add the tomatoes to the saucepan.

6 Add the herbs, salt, and pepper. Stir to blend.

7 Bring the sauce to a boil over medium-high heat, stirring often.

8 Reduce the heat and let the sauce cook over low heat for 1 hour, stirring often.

9 Stir in the brown sugar.

10 Serve this sauce over any cooked pasta.

Fantastic Fettuccine Alfredo

Fettuccine means "little ribbons" in Italian!

MAKES 4 SERVINGS

INGREDIENTS

salt
2 tablespoons butter
1 large shallot, minced
2 cups heavy whipping cream
½ cup grated Parmesan cheese
¼ teaspoon ground pepper
⅛ teaspoon nutmeg
8 ounces fettuccine noodles
¼ cup chopped Italian parsley

TOOLS:

prep bowls	heavy-bottomed saucepan	medium saucepan	strainer
grater		wooden spoon	serving bowl
cutting board	measuring spoons	timer	
small sharp knife	measuring cups	pot holders	

1. Put 4 quarts of water in a large heavy-bottomed saucepan. Add 1 tablespoon of salt. Stir to **dissolve** the salt. Cover the pot and bring the water to a boil.

2. Meanwhile, heat the butter in a medium saucepan over medium-high heat.

3. When the butter is melted, add the shallot. Sauté over medium heat for 3 minutes, stirring with a wooden spoon.

4. Turn down the heat. Stir in the cream, Parmesan cheese, ¼ teaspoon salt, pepper, and nutmeg. Cook over low heat for 5 minutes, stirring often.

5. Add the fettuccine noodles to the boiling water. The package will tell you how long to boil the noodles. See page 16 for more information about cooking pasta.

6. While the fettuccine cooks, continue cooking the sauce over low heat, stirring often.

7. Drain the fettuccine in a strainer. Then put it in a large serving bowl. Pour the sauce over the fettuccine. Stir to coat the pasta with the sauce. Let stand for 5 minutes.

8. Sprinkle with parsley and serve.

Green Beans Parmigiana

Anything with Parmesan cheese can be called Parmigiana!

MAKES 6 SERVINGS

INGREDIENTS

salt

1 pound green beans, ends trimmed off

2 tablespoons butter

2 tablespoons olive oil

½ cup Parmesan cheese, grated

ground pepper

TOOLS:

prep bowls	grater	large saucepan
cutting board	measuring spoons	strainer
small sharp knife	measuring cups	large frying pan
		wooden spoon
		serving bowl

20

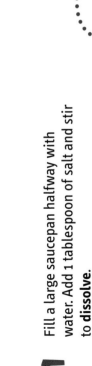

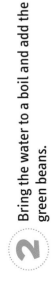

1 Fill a large saucepan halfway with water. Add 1 tablespoon of salt and stir to **dissolve**.

2 Bring the water to a boil and add the green beans.

3 Boil the beans uncovered for 4 to 5 minutes. The beans should be crisp yet tender and bright green.

4 Drain the beans using a strainer. Run cold water over them to stop the cooking process.

5 Put the olive oil and butter in a large frying pan. Heat over medium-high heat until the butter is melted.

6 Add the beans and sauté for 3 minutes, stirring constantly.

7 Put the beans in a serving bowl. Add salt and pepper to taste. Sprinkle with Parmesan cheese and serve.

Legendary Lasagna

Lasagna means "cooking pot" in Latin.
So this dish is named after a dish!

MAKES ABOUT 8 SERVINGS

INGREDIENTS

- 4 cups prepared Remarkable Red Sauce (see page 17)
- 3 cups ricotta cheese
- 2 eggs
- 1 cup Parmesan cheese, grated
- ¼ cup Italian parsley, chopped
- 9-ounce package no-boil lasagna noodles
- 8 ounces mozzarella cheese, grated
- olive oil

TOOLS:

prep bowls	small sharp knife	wooden spoon
grater	measuring cups	9 x 9-inch baking dish
cutting board	mixing bowl	rubber spatula
		aluminum foil
		timer
		pot holders

1. Follow the steps on page 17 to prepare the red sauce. Preheat the oven to 350 degrees.

2. Put the ricotta cheese, eggs, Parmesan cheese, and parsley in a mixing bowl. Mix with a wooden spoon.

3. Spread 1 cup of red sauce evenly over the bottom of the baking dish. Cover the red sauce with a layer of noodles.

4. Spread half the cheese mixture over the noodles. Spread 1 cup of sauce over the cheese mixture.

5. Cover the sauce with a second layer of noodles. Spread the rest of the cheese mixture over the noodles.

6. Spread 1 cup of red sauce over the cheese mixture. Cover the red sauce with a third layer of noodles. Spread 1 cup of red sauce over the noodles. Sprinkle the mozzarella cheese evenly over the top.

7. Cut a piece of aluminum foil large enough to cover the dish. Rub olive oil on one side. Put the foil oil side down over the dish. Press it tightly around the edges. Bake covered for 45 minutes.

8. Remove the foil. Continue baking for 15 more minutes. It should be bubbly around the edges. Test the center to make sure it is hot all the way through. Ask an adult to help you. Remove the lasagna from the oven. Let it stand for 10 minutes before serving.

Even Cooler!

Don't have time for homemade sauce? Buy a jar of red sauce to use instead!

Marvelous Meatballs

Add some red sauce and pasta for a magnificent meal!

MAKES 4 SERVINGS

TOOLS:

cutting board
small sharp knife
prep bowls

measuring cups
measuring spoons
grater

large mixing bowl
baking sheet
pot holders

timer
large saucepan

24

INGREDIENTS

4 cups prepared Remarkable Red Sauce, sausage left out (see page 17)

½ pound ground beef

½ pound bulk Italian sausage

½ cup bread crumbs

1 egg

¼ cup chopped fresh Italian parsley

½ cup grated Parmesan cheese

2 cloves garlic, minced

¾ teaspoon salt

ground pepper

1 lb. prepared spaghetti noodles (see page 16)

1. Follow the steps on page 17 to prepare the red sauce. Don't add the sausage. Preheat the oven to 400 degrees.

2. Put all the remaining ingredients except the noodles in a large mixing bowl. Using your hands, blend all the ingredients together. Wash your hands first!

3. Get your hands wet. Roll some of the mixture between your hands to make a meatball. It should be about 1½ inches across.

4. Put the meatball on a baking sheet. Make more meatballs until you have used all of the mixture. Bake the meatballs for 25 minutes.

5. Check the meatballs for doneness. Cut one in half. Make sure it is not still pink inside. If the meatballs are not done, bake for 5 more minutes.

6. Combine the meatballs and the red sauce in a large saucepan. Cook over medium heat for 30 minutes.

7. Meanwhile, prepare the spaghetti noodles. Follow the steps on page 16.

Tip

You can make the meatballs ahead of time! Then store them in the refrigerator in a zip top bag. You need to use them within a day or two. Or you can freeze the meatballs for up to three months. Wrap the zip top bag in two layers of aluminum foil. When you are ready to use the meatballs, let them thaw in the refrigerator for 24 hours. Then follow step 6 to reheat them in the sauce.

Impressive Insalata Mista

Italy's version of a mixed salad!

MAKES 6-8 SERVINGS

INGREDIENTS

1 garlic clove, cut in half

1 head Bibb lettuce, washed and dried

1 red bell pepper, cut into thin strips

4 scallions, chopped

6 ounces field greens

1 stalk celery, cut into thin slices

2 carrots, peeled and grated using largest holes on grater

1 tablespoon fresh lemon juice

3 tablespoons olive oil

2 tomatoes, cut into wedges

2 teaspoons red wine vinegar

salt

ground pepper

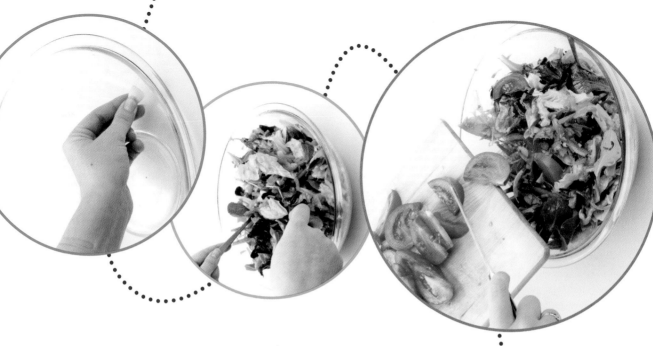

1. Rub a large salad bowl with the garlic. Leave the garlic in the bowl.

2. Put the lettuce in the bowl. Tear it into bite-size pieces. Add the bell pepper, scallions, field greens, celery, and carrots.

3. Sprinkle the lemon juice over the salad and toss gently to mix. Sprinkle the olive oil over the salad and toss again.

4. Add the tomatoes. Sprinkle red wine vinegar over the salad. Toss gently to mix.

5. Remove the garlic. Add salt and pepper to taste. Serve immediately.

Even Cooler!

Try using other types of lettuce such as butter lettuce, Romaine lettuce, or leaf lettuce. You could also use cherry tomatoes instead of whole tomatoes. Or add sliced radishes, green bell pepper, or mushrooms.

Tangy Lemon Granita

It takes six hours, but every bite is worth it!

MAKES 6 SERVINGS

TOOLS:

prep bowl	small saucepan	pot holders	fork
juicer	wooden spoon	round glass baking dish	dessert bowls
measuring cups	timer		

28

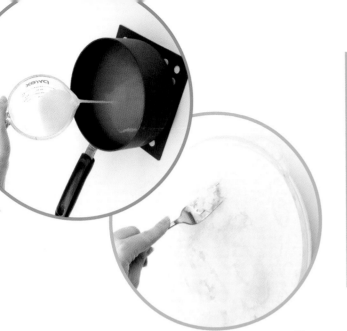

1 Start making the granita at least six hours before serving. Put the water and sugar in a small saucepan over high heat. Use a wooden spoon to stir until the sugar is **dissolved**.

2 Bring the mixture to a boil and cook for 5 minutes. Remove the pan from the heat. Let the mixture stand for 5 minutes.

3 Add the lemon juice and stir to mix. Let the mixture cool for 20 minutes.

4 Pour the mixture into the baking dish. Put the dish in the freezer.

5 Remove the dish from the freezer after 2 hours. The mixture will be slushy. Use a fork to mash it and mix the frozen and unfrozen parts. Put the dish back in the freezer.

6 Repeat the mashing and mixing every hour for the next 4 hours. Put it in dessert bowls to serve.

Even Cooler!

Try making granita with juice from oranges or pink grapefruit. You can also make granita from bottled juice. If the juice is already sweetened, pour it into the baking dish. Begin at step 4.

Tip

You can make the granita ahead of time. After Step 6, leave the granita in the baking dish. Cover the dish with plastic wrap. Put it back in the freezer. Take it out 15 minutes before you want to serve the granita. Use a fork to mash and mix one more time. Then put it in the dessert bowls.

Wrap it Up!

Now you know how to make **delicious** Italian dishes! What did you learn? Did you try any new foods? Learning about recipes from around the world teaches you a lot. You learn about different **cultures**, climates, geography, and tastes.

Making international dishes also teaches you about new languages. Did you learn any new Italian words in this book? These new words will help you sound like a native speaker. You'll be able to use them at restaurants and **grocery stores.**

Insalata Mista (EEN-sah-LAH-tah MEE-stah)

Granita (grah-NEE-tah)

Parmigiana (pahr-muh-ZHAH-nuh)

Lasagna (luh-ZAHN-yuh)

Napoli (NAH-poh-lee)

Glossary

conventionally – in the usual way.

cousin – the child of your aunt or uncle.

culture – the behavior, beliefs, art, and other products of a particular group of people.

dangerous – able or likely to cause harm or injury.

delicious – very pleasing to taste or smell.

dissolve – to become part of a liquid.

grocery store – a place where you buy food items.

nutritious – good for people to eat.

optional – something you can choose, but is not required.

pesticide – a chemical used to kills bugs and other pests.

synthetic – man-made rather than found in nature.

towel – a cloth or paper used for cleaning or drying.

version – a different form or type from the original.

Web Sites

To learn more about cool cooking, visit ABDO Publishing Company on the World Wide Web at **www.abdopublishing.com**. Web sites about cool cooking are featured on our Book Links page. These links are routinely monitored and updated to provide the most current information available.

Index